Real
Relationships
WORKBOOK

Resources by Les and Leslie Parrott

Books

Becoming Soul Mates
The Complete Guide to Marriage Mentoring
Dot.com Dating
Getting Ready for the Wedding
I Love You More (and workbooks)*
Just the Two of Us
L.O.V.E. (and workbooks)*
Love Is . . .
The Love List
Love Talk (and workbooks)*
Meditations on Proverbs for Couples
The Parent You Want to Be*
Pillow Talk
Questions Couples Ask
Real Relationships (and workbook)
Saving Your Marriage Before It Starts (and workbooks)*
Saving Your Second Marriage Before It Starts (and workbooks)*
Trading Places (and workbooks)*
Your Time-Starved Marriage (and workbooks)*
51 Creative Ideas for Marriage Mentors

Video Curriculum—ZondervanGroupware®

Complete Resource Kit for Marriage Mentoring
I Love You More
Love Talk
Saving Your Marriage Before It Starts

Books by Les Parrott

The Control Freak
Crazy Good Sex*
Helping Your Struggling Teenager
High Maintenance Relationships
The Life You Want Your Kids to Live
Seven Secrets of a Healthy Dating Relationship
Shoulda, Coulda, Woulda*
Once Upon a Family
3 Seconds*
25 Ways to Win with People (coauthored with John Maxwell)
Love the Life You Live (coauthored with Neil Clark Warren)

Books by Leslie Parrott

The First Drop of Rain*
If You Ever Needed Friends, It's Now
You Matter More Than You Think*
God Loves You Nose to Toes (children's book)
Marshmallow Clouds (children's book)

•Audio version available

Real
Relationships
W O R K B O O K

From Bad
to Better
and Good
to Great

DRS. LES & LESLIE
PARROTT

Previously published as Relationships Workbook

ZONDERVAN.com/
AUTHORTRACKER
follow your favorite authors

ZONDERVAN

Real Relationships Workbook
Copyright © 2011 by Les and Leslie Parrott

Previously published as *Relationships Workbook*
Copyright © 1998 by Les and Leslie Parrott

This title is also available as a Zondervan ebook.
Visit www.zondervan.com/ebooks.

Requests for information should be addressed to:
Zondervan, *Grand Rapids, Michigan 49530*

ISBN 978-0-310-33446-0

Published in association with Yates & Yates, www.yates2.com.

Cover design: Extra Credit Projects
Cover photography: iStockphoto®
Interior design: Beth Shagene

Printed in the United States of America

11 12 13 14 15 16 17 18 /DCI/ 24 23 22 21 20 19 18 17 16 15 14 13 12 11 10 9 8 7 6 5 4 3 2 1

Contents

CHAPTER 4: Friends to Die For
Exercises

CHAPTER 5: What to Do When Friends Fail
Exercises

CHAPTER 6: Falling in Love without Losing Your Mind
Exercises

CHAPTER 7: Sex, Lies, and the Great Escape
Exercises

CHAPTER 8: How to Break Up without Falling Apart
               Exercises

CHAPTER 9: Relating to God without Feeling Phony
               Exercises

**For Group Discussion
with the Accompanying DVD**

How to Use This Workbook

Too often, reading a book can lead to great ideas, but little action. This workbook is meant to change all that. Its self-tests and exercises will help you put feet on the ideas you have while reading *Real Relationships*. And we believe you'll enjoy it. As Shakespeare said, "Joy's soul lies in the doing."

While this workbook will become a rather personal record of your own exploration—and while it is designed to be used on your own—we have also written it to be used in group settings. In other words, you may want to do the self-tests and exercises while reading each chapter on your own, and then take time to discuss the questions with others after completing the chapter (this makes for a convenient classroom or small group series). In fact, we highly recommend this. Interacting with others on this material will not only help you compare and contrast your varying viewpoints, it will help you better define and articulate your own perspective. In other words, to maximize this material, study it with other people. After all, this book is about relationships!

In addition to the book *Real Relationships* and this accompanying workbook, we have produced two additional tools we think you may want to consider—especially if you're going through this material with other people.

1. **The *Real Relationships* DVD**. This little series provides several ten-minute sessions to help you jump-start your group interaction. Each lively session is designed to pull your group more personally into the material and help them share from the heart.

2. **The Small Group Insights Online Tool**. If you have a copy of *Real Relationships* (the book) you already know that it comes with a complimentary code to use this online tool. After answering a few questions (less than ten minutes), it provides you with a personalized report on your "relationship style." We think you'll really find this helpful. And it's sure to become a great catalyst for meaningful dialogue. If you don't have a

code or would like additional codes to use the tool, you can easily obtain them at **www.SmallGroupInsights.com**.

Whether you use this workbook on your own or in a group, we want you to know that each chapter of this workbook contains four specific self-tests or exercises to tap into a particular idea you are reading about. We suggest pausing as you make your way through each chapter and doing the recommended exercises at that particular time. Each section concludes with suggestions for a brief study of Scripture as it relates to the chapter's topic.

As you work through the pages of this book, make it your own. Don't get too hung up on following the rules. If a particular exercise leads you down a more intriguing path, take it. Some of these exercises may simply serve as springboards to discussions that more appropriately fit your style. However, if an exercise seems a bit challenging, don't give up on it. As the saying goes, anything worth having is worth working for. In any case, we pray you will enjoy your journey toward making bad relationships better and good relationships great.

LES AND LESLIE PARROTT
Center for Relationship Development
Seattle Pacific University

The Compulsion for Completion Exercises

Your Relational Readiness

The following self-test will take about five minutes and will help you assess your relational "readiness." Answer each item by using the following scale to indicate the degree to which it is true for you:

4 — Often
3 — Sometimes
2 — Rarely
1 — Never

_____ I feel a sense of relief when I don't have to be alone.

_____ Any relationship is better than nothing.

_____ If I'm not in a dating relationship, I feel less desirable.

_____ I experience a little bit of panic when I think of not having someone to be close to.

_____ The very idea of solitude strikes fear in my heart.

_____ I'm tempted to settle for most any relationship because I don't know if I can find anyone better.

_____ My romantic relationships are more of an issue of being selected rather than doing the selecting.

_____ When I am dating someone I feel better about myself.

_____ I don't like to be alone.

_____ I don't have a very clear idea of the personal qualities I look for in a person to date or even to be friends with.

_____ TOTAL SCORE

continued next page

Scoring: Add the numbers you have placed beside each item. There is a possible total of forty points. To interpret your score, use the following scale:

40–30   A score in this range is a strong indicator of your need to establish a healthier sense of your identity and personal wholeness. You will want to pay special attention to the four steps toward wholeness discussed in this chapter.

29–20   A score in this range indicates that you have done some significant work in establishing a healthy identity and a good sense of self-worth. You still have more work to do, however, in constructing an integrated and whole sense of self that will help to ensure healthier relationships.

19–1   A score in this range indicates an established sense of security in who you are and a confident perspective on your sense of personal wholeness. This should serve you well in your relationships.

Healing Your Primal Pain

This exercise can take as little as fifteen minutes, or it can take much longer. You will require a place for quiet contemplation and self-exploration, and you may want to use additional paper for this exercise.

• Reflect on your personal history and make note of any memories you have of feeling abandoned or neglected (even if they seem fairly insignificant).

• Are there people from your past or present that you blame for not being there for you? Who are they and what do you blame them for?

- As you review these painful moments from your past, do you see ways in which they may still be impacting your present? In what ways are they determining choices you are making when it comes to your relationships?

- Are you able to forgive whoever is involved in your painful memories? Are you able to release any resentment you may be holding onto? What might you need to do to take care of your "unfinished business"?

If you are carrying a great deal of personal pain from your past and not finding resolution for it in the present, you could probably benefit greatly from seeking the help of a trusted friend, minister, or counselor.

EXERCISE 3

Taking Off Your Masks

This exercise will take about ten minutes and will help you become more aware of the masks you sometimes use to guard against feeling judged or negatively evaluated. It focuses on three areas: work, home, and church; if you'd like to add another, feel free.

I wear masks at work (or school):

Very Often   Almost Never

If your answer was between one and four, describe the kinds of masks you wear at work (or school) and with whom.

I wear masks at home:

Very Often   Almost Never

If your answer was between one and four, describe the kinds of masks you wear at home and with whom.

I wear masks at church:

Very Often   Almost Never

If your answer was between one and four, describe the kinds of masks you wear at church and with whom.

Now review your responses and determine which of your masks serves a helpful function and which ones you think may be interfering with your ability to cultivate healthy relationships. What can you do to discard these unhealthy masks?

Designing Your Destiny

This exercise will take about fifteen minutes or more. It is designed to help you construct a personal statement of purpose and create goals that will help you fulfill it.

To begin with, take a moment to determine what you value. It will be difficult, but force yourself to rank the following twelve values (1 = most important to you).

_____ **Achievement:** Feeling satisfaction for a job well done

_____ **Challenges:** Using your creativity, training, and intelligence to face challenges

_____ **Education:** Increasing your intellectual understanding of life

_____ **Aesthetic Considerations:** Appreciating the beauty in people, art, or nature

_____ **Health:** Feeling good in a physical and emotional sense

_____ **Independence:** Having freedom to do your own thing

_____ **Morality:** Maintaining your moral, ethical, and religious standards

_____ **Pleasure:** Having time to play and have a good time

_____ **Relationships:** Caring for, sharing with, and giving to those who are close to you

_____ **Spirituality:** Cultivating a meaningful and personal relationship with God

_____ **Security:** Feeling safe, free from unexpected and unpleasant changes

_____ **Service to Others:** Knowing you have benefited others

_____ **Wealth:** Improving your financial position

As you ponder what matters most to you, consider how your top three or four values can be incorporated into a personal purpose statement. This statement does not need to be permanent (it will change throughout your life). Just draft something that seems right for you at this time—something that is personally compelling and comes from the heart.

My purpose is . . .

Once you've drafted your purpose statement, note some specific and obtainable goals that can serve as a means to fulfill it.

Short-term goals (obtainable within the next three or four months):

1.

2.

3.

Long-term goals (obtainable within the next year or more):

1.

2.

3.

In what specific ways will you need to delay your immediate gratification in order to enjoy the benefits of meeting your goals?

The Compulsion for Completion

To explore more of what the Bible has to say about this topic, consider the following passages and use the space provided to jot down your thoughts and notes:

- 1 John 4:7–21 talks about how our love for one another is predicated on God's love of us.

- Colossians 1:19–22 talks about how God accepts us like no human can.

- Ephesians 4:14 and 2 Corinthians 10:7 talk about our feeble attempts to find significance in surface things.

CHAPTER 2

Keeping Family Ties from Pulling Strings Exercises

How Healthy Is Your Home?

This exercise will take about ten minutes and will help you assess the health of your home. Understand that no family is perfect. But some families are healthier than others. In fact, Dolores Curran, in her book *Traits of a Healthy Family* (Ballantine, 1983), unveils the results of a study identifying the top fifteen traits noted again and again by family experts. They are noted below.

Using the following scale, rate the degree to which your family is character-ized by these desirable traits.

4 — Much of the time
3 — Some of the time
2 — Rarely
1 — Almost never

_____ Communicates and listens

_____ Affirms and supports one another

_____ Teaches respect for others

_____ Develops a sense of trust

_____ Has a sense of play and humor

_____ Exhibits a sense of shared responsibility

_____ Teaches a sense of right and wrong

_____ Has a strong sense of family in which rituals and traditions abound

_____ Has a balance of interaction among members

_____ Has a shared religious core

_____ Respects the privacy of one another

_____ Values service to others

2 Keeping Family Ties from Pulling Strings Exercises

_____ Fosters family table time and conversation

_____ Shares leisure time

_____ Admits to and seeks help with problems

_____ TOTAL SCORE

Scoring: Add the numbers you have placed beside each item. There is a possible total of sixty points. To interpret your score, use the following:

50–60 Count your blessings. You grew up in a relatively loving home free of dysfunction. Mom and Dad took time to nurture your development and cultivate an atmosphere that was positive and caring. Your relationships will certainly benefit from this good foundation.

30–49 Your family health falls into the midrange, or average zone. Your family may not be all you'd like it to be, but then again, things could be a lot worse. You will want to learn from the tensions and disengaged style that is sometimes present in your home. How do you contribute to it, and what can you do to make the relationships better?

1–29 This range, unfortunately, is where you will find families with the most strife. Perhaps you have experienced a lot of distressed and polarized relationships (even abusive ones) at home. If so, this will present some challenges to your present and future relationships, but nothing that can't be overcome with good relational skills.

Uncovering Unspoken Rules

This exercise will take about ten or fifteen minutes and will help you pin-point the unspoken rules you absorbed from your family of origin.

Take your time to complete the following sentence stems. Simply complete them by writing the first thing that pops into your head:

• Men should . . .

• Women should . . .

• Success is . . .

• The most important thing . . .

• Life . . .

Now review what you have written and edit it to conform to how you believe your parents would have completed these sentences. This will give you a pretty good start at uncovering your family's unspoken rules. Use the space below to write down any additional rules that may not have been articulated, but were still known.

In what specific ways will your family's unspoken rules influence your relationships?

Lessons Learned from Mom and Dad

We all learn by example, especially when that example is Mom and Dad. In the following relationship skill areas, note how each of your parents (or primary caretakers) behaved. You might rate their effectiveness on a scale of one to ten (one being "not very effective," and ten being "very effective") and then write a brief description of how each performed in that skill. This exercise will take about ten to fifteen minutes.

	Your Mother	Your Father
Talking about their experiences		
Showing their feelings		
Standing up for themselves		
Being a good listener		
Understanding other's perspective		
Managing anger		
Accepting responsibility (not passing the buck)		
Working for equitable solutions		

If Your Parents Got Divorced

This exercise will take about ten minutes and will help you apply the principles discussed in the chapter.

Take a moment to list the things you have done to come to terms with your parents' divorce. In specific terms, what have you done to bring personal healing to the pain it has caused you? What things have helped the most?

How well are you managing your anger?

Not so well   Very Well

1   2   3   4   5   6   7

If this is not going so well, what specific steps can you take to get your anger under control?

How well are you managing conflict-avoidance?

Not so well   Very Well

If this is not going so well, what specific steps can you take to express your genuine feelings — even when they may cause conflict?

How would you rate the strength of your self-confidence?

Not so strong   Very strong

If your self-confidence is not too strong, what specific steps can you take to build it up?

As you review this exercise, consider your overall health in the aftermath of your parents' divorce. If it is not getting better for you, we urge you to seek help from a competent counselor, a compassionate minister, or even a concerned friend. The strength of all your other relationships depends on it.

Keeping Family Ties from Pulling Strings

To explore more of what the Bible has to say about this topic, consider the following passages:

• 1 Kings 22 is just one biblical example of how powerful the family's impact is.

• Ephesians 5:21 – 33 talks about the relationship of husbands and wives, the architects of every family.

- Romans 8:28 gives encouraging words for everyone who has not had the greatest home life.

CHAPTER 3

Crossing the Gender Line Exercises

What's Your Gender I.Q.?

This exercise will take about five minutes and will help you get a general idea of how much you already know about some fundamental differences between the genders. Answer each of the following items as either true or false.

1. T F Women are better spellers than men.

2. T F Men are more likely than women to use conversation to solve problems.

3. T F Women have larger connections between their brain's left and right hemispheres.

4. T F Men are better at reading the emotions of others than women are.

5. T F Men score higher on the math section of the SAT than do women.

6. T F In comparison to men, women are better at maintaining a sense of geographical direction.

7. T F Men are better than women at fitting suitcases into a crowded car trunk.

8. T F Women are better than men at describing their feelings.

9. T F Men, more than women, focus their energy on achievement.

10. T F Women, more than men, give priority to relationships.

Scoring: Each of these items is based on current gender research studies. Note how many of the items you got correct. 1-T, 2-T, 3-T, 4-F, 5-T, 6-F, 7-T, 8-T, 9-T, 10-T. The higher your score, the better your base knowledge of gender differences.

What If You Were the Opposite Sex?

This exercise can take as little as fifteen minutes to much longer. As strange and as difficult as this might seem, do your best to imagine what it would be like to live as the opposite sex. In other words, if you are a man, what would life be like for you if you were a woman? And if you are a woman, what would it be like to live as a man? With this in mind, answer the following questions as honestly as you can.

1. What is your first reaction to living as the opposite sex?

2. How would the simple task of getting ready in the morning be different if you were the opposite gender (e.g., the time it would take, what you would do, how you would dress)?

3. How would living as the opposite sex affect your career choice and other aspirations?

4. As the opposite gender, would you feel more or less safe in society? Why?

5. Would you feel any different about dating and the prospect of marriage if you were the opposite gender? If so, how?

6. How would your relationship with both your mom and dad differ if you were the opposite gender?

Once you have taken the time to answer these questions, you may find it insightful to share your answers with another person who has completed the same exercise.

A Self-Test for Women Only

This exercise will take about ten minutes and will help you review and apply some important insights in understanding the men in your life. Take a moment to reflect on what the book has to say about "what women need to know about men." For each of the statements below, note an example from your own life that illustrates the point.

• Men are not as in touch with their emotions as we are.

• Men are more independent than we are.

- Men are more abstract than we are.

Next, consider what you can do in practical terms to bridge the gender gap with the most important men in your life. In other words, how can you apply the above insights to these relationships?

A Self-Test for Men Only

This exercise will take about ten minutes and will help you review and apply some important insights in understanding the women in your life. Take a moment to reflect on what the book has to say about "what men need to know about women." For each of the statements below, note an example from your own life that illustrates the point.

• Women are not as independent as we are.

• Women focus on the here-and-now more than we do.

- Women are not as competitive as we are.

Next, consider what you can do in practical terms to bridge the gender gap with the most important women in your life. In other words, how can you apply the above insights to these relationships?

Crossing the Gender Line

To explore more of what the Bible has to say about this topic, consider the following passages:

- Genesis 1:27 talks of both male and female being created in the image of God.

- Galatians 3:28 instructs us in the equality and unity of the genders before God in Christ.

- Ephesians 4:4–8 reminds us that although we each have been given different gifts, we are one in Christ.

CHAPTER 4

Friends to Die For Exercises

The Friendship Assessment

This exercise will help you evaluate the current condition of each of your friendships. It will take about ten minutes or so, depending on how many friendships you evaluate.

Have a specific friend in mind and then answer each of the following true and false questions as honestly as you can.

T   F   This person knows how to keep a secret.

T   F   We can disagree and then make up without holding grudges.

T   F   This person almost always makes time for me, and I do the same for him/her.

T   F   When he/she gives me advice, it is generally without judgment.

T   F   I can totally be myself around this person.

T   F   He/she is a good listener.

T   F   This person has stuck by me through tough times and is willing to make personal sacrifices for me.

T   F   This person knows my faults, but loves me anyway.

T   F   Our relationship is balanced with give and take; we are equally vulnerable and caring.

T   F   I am able to set clear boundaries with this person when necessary, and he/she respects them.

T   F   No subject is off-limits in our conversation.

T   F   I can always count on this person.

_____   TOTAL NUMBER OF "T" RESPONSES FOR . . .

4 Friends to Die For Exercises

_____ TOTAL NUMBER OF "T" RESPONSES FOR . . .

_____ TOTAL NUMBER OF "T" RESPONSES FOR . . .

_____ TOTAL NUMBER OF "T" RESPONSES FOR . . .

Scoring: Add up the number of true responses you have for each friendship you evaluated. There is a possible total of twelve points for each relationship. To interpret your score, use the following:

10–12   No doubt about it, this is a good friend who is worth all the effort, care, and investment. You will want to do all that you can to nurture this relationship and enjoy it.

7–9   Although this person could be more sensitive to your needs, this amigo shows great potential. Be careful, however, not to set yourself up for disappointment if this person doesn't meet all your expectations.

0–6   This friend is probably too fair-weather to see you through stormy times (and maybe even the sunny ones, too). Don't hang all your hopes on this one.

Are You a "Growth Promoting" Listener?

Most of us have a lot of room for improvement when it comes to learning to listen. This exercise will help you assess your strengths and areas for growth when it comes to this important friendship skill. It will take about five or ten minutes.

It is important that you be honest in answering each of the following three items. Each one asks you about one of the primary aspects of what Carl Rogers called "growth promoting" listening. Simply circle the number that most accurately indicates where you would be on the continuums.

Generally speaking, in meeting someone for the first time at a party, are you *genuinely* interested in getting to know them and understanding their story? Do you really want to know what interests them? Or are you more likely to just go through the motions, being socially appropriate but not very genuine?

Not Genuine   Extremely Genuine

Generally speaking, in meeting someone for the first time at a party, are you *accepting* of that person's opinions and feelings? Do you feel open to hearing what they have to say, or are you more likely to interject your opinions and feelings before completely understanding theirs?

Not Accepting   Extremely Accepting

Generally speaking, in meeting someone for the first time at a party, are you *empathic* with them? Do you put yourself in their shoes and try to accurately understand their experience, or are you more likely to jump to a few conclusions and make a few assumptions?

Not Empathic   Extremely Empathic

1   2   3   4   5   6   7

_____ TOTAL SCORE

Scoring and Interpretation: Add up the numbers you have circled. There is a total of twenty-one points possible, and the higher your score, the more likely you are to be a "growth promoting" listener. However, you may find it most helpful to consider each continuum separately to see which of the three important qualities you will want to work on most.

Are You a Fair-Weather Friend?

This exercise will take about five minutes and will help you assess how loyal you are to your friends. Consider what your friends would say about you when it comes to the following statements. Answer yes or no to each of these items and be as honest as you can.

My friends would say . . .

Y N   I always keep my promises.

Y N   I always stick up for them.

Y N   I give them grace when they let me down.

Y N   I am just as likely to genuinely celebrate my friends' successes as I am to comfort them in their disappointments.

Y N   I am there when they need me.

Y N   I am ready and willing to lend them a hand.

Y N   I never gossip about them or talk behind their back.

Y N   I give them the benefit of the doubt.

Y N   I hear them out even when I disagree.

Y N   I stand by them through thick and thin.

Scoring: The more items you honestly responded to with a yes, the more likely you are to be loyal to your friends. If you answered yes to nearly all of the items, however, you probably shouldn't take this quality in yourself for granted. Check in with your pals. Ask them to give you a loyalty checkup by inviting them for honest feedback on how you are doing with being loyal. On the other hand, if you did not answer yes to very many of these items, you may want to talk to your friends about how you can better cultivate this quality. Remember, loyalty tops the list of what people appreciate most about their friends, so this is one you will want to spend some time on.

Determining Your Dedication Quotient

How dedicated are you to your friends? This exercise will help you answer this question. It will take as little as ten minutes to much longer, depending on whether you discuss your answers with another person who has done the same exercise.

Consider your closest friendships and think about them as you put yourself in the following scenarios. Indicate how you would respond, and feel free to write your own response to better capture what you would say.

Scenario One

You get a call from one of your good friends at 2:00 a.m. He recently called it quits with someone he has been dating for several months, and now he is having second thoughts.

Do you say . . .

a. "I can't believe you're calling me at 2:00 a.m. I've got to sleep."

b. "I am so sorry, but I can't even think clearly at this hour. Let's meet over breakfast."

c. "Tell me how you're doing."

d. Other: _____

Scenario Two

One of your good friends is moving to a new apartment on Saturday and asks you to help out by lending a hand and also loaning your car. You have an important project due on Monday and you were planning on using your weekend to do it. You're also not that crazy about using your car as a moving van.

Do you say . . .

a. "I'd love to help you, but there is just no possible way."

b. "I can help you for a couple of hours in the morning, but I've got to work on my project in the afternoon."

c. "No problem. Whatever it takes to help a friend."

d. Other: _____

Scenario Three

One of your good friends shows interest in dating someone you had once dated seriously (for about six months). You currently have no attachments to this person, but you have uneasy feelings about the two of them getting together. Your friend asks you how you feel about it.

Do you say . . .

a. "If you go out, I don't see how we can still be friends."

b. "Sure, I don't mind." (And secretly resent it.)

c. "To be honest, I have funny feelings about it, but I'm not sure why."

d. Other: _____

The point of this exercise is to get you thinking about your level of dedication to your friendships. None of the answers is the only "right" one; there is no objective score to be obtained. You may, however, find it helpful to compare your responses with someone else to get some objective feedback. Ask each other why you chose the answers you did and whether you feel good about them. Consider whether you are more dedicated in certain areas (e.g., during times of immediate crisis) than you are in others. And why you are more dedicated to some friends than you are to others. Finally, if you are feeling like your dedication level is lacking, explore concrete ways you can improve it.

You've Got a Virtual Friend in Me

Social networking and technology allow us to enrich the connections we have with our friends, but if we are not careful, this technology can also inhibit our relationships.

On the following scale, which side would be heaviest for you? Write the rough percentage on each side of the scale:

| 100% | 50% | 0% | 50% | 100% |

Maintain meaningful connections with real friends

Distract me from meaningful in-person connections

What are the three most important benefits for you when it comes to social networking?

1.

2.

3.

As you learned in the chapter, we need to be cautious with these tools and how they impact our real relationships. What are your three biggest challenges when it comes to technology and social networking — three things that hinder your real friendships — and why?

1.

2.

3.

What is one action-step you can take to be more intentional in using (or not using) social networking to be sure your real relationships are prioritized?

Quick reality check: What's your primary motivation for having virtual friends? Is it a means to stay in touch with "real" friends? Is it a sign of popularity to you? Do you ever feel competitive in having more virtual friends than others do?

Friends to Die For

To explore more of what the Bible has to say about this topic, consider the following passages:

- Ruth 1:1 – 18 talks about a woman who went far beyond what was expected for a friend.

- Job 2:1 – 13 talks about how true friendship offers comfort when the pain is beyond understanding.

- 2 Timothy 1:1 – 18 talks about the importance of encouragement in strengthening friendship.

CHAPTER 5

What to Do When Friends Fail Exercises

What You Expect from Friends

This exercise will take about five minutes and will help you clarify what you expect from your closest friends. Answer the following true-and-false items as honestly as you can.

T F I expect my friend to know my faults but accept me anyway.

T F I expect my friend to never break special plans with me — even for a date at the last minute.

T F I expect my close friends to always keep their word on both big and small issues.

T F A really good friend should know how I'm feeling most of the time.

T F I expect my friend to say "I'm sorry" when he or she is wrong.

T F My closest friend should confide in me more than anyone else.

T F I expect my friend to always keep a secret.

T F It is difficult for me to forgive a friend who has hurt me in some way.

T F If we are truly friends, we should hardly ever have much conflict.

T F I expect my friends to never talk behind my back or break a confidence — even about small things.

T F My very closest friend should have no other friendships closer than ours.

T F If a good friend breaks a confidence or fails me in some other way, I am unlikely to give him or her a second or third chance.

T F I expect my friend to never hold a grudge against me.

T F   I expect my friend to always admit when he or she is wrong.

If you answered true to any of these items, you are more likely to have very high standards about how your friends should treat you. The more times you answered true, the more you expect from your friends and perhaps the more rigid you are with your expectations.

Learning from Your Own Failed Friendships

This exercise can take as little as ten minutes. It is designed to help you gain insight into how you can avoid repeating patterns of painful relationships. Take your time as you consider a relationship where a person you trusted failed you in some way, and answer the following questions to help you learn from the failure.

• How long did you know this person, and what brought you together?

• Looking back over your relationship, what kinds of things helped you to believe you could trust him or her?

• In specific terms, what did this person do to "fail" you?

- What percentage of the hurt was due to the following:

Percentage

_____ miscommunication

_____ broken confidence

_____ gossip

_____ neglect

_____ betrayal

_____ uncontrollable change (moving)

_____ personality change

_____ moral choices

_____ other _____

- Take a moment for some serious soul searching and try to assess how much you were responsible for the falling out with this friend. Was there anything you did or didn't do that may have contributed to the problem? If so, what was it?

- Did you ever want to get revenge as a result of the hurt you felt from this relationship, and if so, why? Also, what did you do with your vengeful feelings and what was the result?

- Have you come to a place of healing with the hurt you experienced? If so, what helped bring this about?

- In reviewing the basis for your relationship and the reasons for your fallout, what can you surmise about how to avoid a similar situation in future friendships?

Can This Friendship Be Saved?

This exercise will take about five to ten minutes and is designed to help you assess the status of an increasingly troublesome friendship. Consider your particular relationship and take a moment to answer yes or no to the following questions.

Y N You find that one of you is always saying, after the other says hello, "Sorry I didn't get back to you; I've been so busy."

Y N You make a date with a friend and later schedule another appointment at the same time without realizing it.

Y N You find you talk more about your friend to others than you talk to your friend.

Y N When you get together with your friend, you find yourself sitting silently, refusing to ask how she is, and you realize that you're waiting for her to first ask you how you are; it doesn't happen.

Y N You don't like yourself after you've been with him, because he can bring out the worst in you.

Y N You realize that you no longer feel safe being completely honest with her about your personal life.

Y N You're losing patience with his chronic lateness and are frequently mumbling "I've had it" under your breath.

Y N You've reminisced about the past for the fifth straight time and realize that there's an increasing lack of current history between you.

Y N You've talked to your friend about how you feel hurt or neglected and yet there are no signs of positive change.

Y   N   You feel forced by the relationship to compromise your principles or subvert your self-respect.

_____ NUMBER OF YES RESPONSES

If you circled yes on three or more of the above statements, your friendship needs work. But unfortunately, it might be beyond repair. Some betrayals are just too big to forgive and forget. Some friendships are so flawed they constantly weigh you down. Other times friends simply outgrow each other. While no one but you can make the decision whether or not to end a friendship, if you've circled yes on most of the above items, you shouldn't ignore the option.

Making Amends

This exercise can take as much as fifteen minutes or longer. While it may appear to be somewhat rigid or systematic, please do not let it keep you from doing whatever your heart is telling you to do to make amends with the person you care about. Consider these steps as guidelines to help you bring healing and restoration to a floundering friendship.

STEP ONE: Count the Cost

What is the price you are paying to keep this friendship alive? If you were forced to choose between the following two statements, which one would best describe how you feel about this friendship?

1. This friendship has redeeming qualities I value and is worth the cost of repairing and maintaining.
2. This friendship is unhealthy and forces me to compromise my convictions.

If you chose the second statement, it is time to make a clean break. If you chose the first statement, you are ready to make amends by progressing to the next step.

STEP TWO: Make Meaningful Contact

You now need to determine the best way to convey the following message to your friend: "Our friendship is valuable to me, and I miss seeing you. Is there any way we can resolve what stands between us?" Knowing your friend as you do, would it be best to convey this message in writing (with a brief note), on the phone, or in person? Once you determine the means, take care to send the right message by cleaning your heart and mind of lingering desires to get back at your friend. Take a moment right now to note what has hurt you and how you may still want to get even. Be honest with yourself about your anger and feelings of revenge.

STEP THREE: Forgive as Best You Can

Once you have a handle on your hurt and angry feelings, you will need to do your best to step beyond them by trying to forgive. This is not an easy step, but it is vital to making amends. It begins by putting yourself in your friend's shoes and seeing the relationship and situation from his or her perspective.

• How do you imagine your friend feels about what is going on between the two of you?

• Is your friend feeling as hurt as you are? If so, why?

- If the roles were reversed, how do you think the relationship would be different?

- Knowing that hardly any relationship problem is ever entirely one person's fault, what do you take responsibility for in this situation?

- Are you able and willing to set aside your pride and give grace to your friend? If so, how can you do this?

STEP FOUR: Diagnose the Problem

Once you have come to a place where you can forgive your friend and convey the simple message of wanting to make things right, the two of you may need to explore together why the problem emerged so that it won't happen again. It's up to the two of you to determine whether this step of having an honest discussion of differences is necessary.

STEP FIVE: Rebuild Respect

This last step is critical to making amends. Ask yourself what traits your friend possesses that inspire you to become a better person and then make a list of a half dozen of your friend's most admirable qualities.

1.

2.

3.

4.

5.

6.

Now that you have made this list, you are ready to offer a sincere apology to your friend and express to him or her just how important the relationship is to you and how much you appreciate his or her qualities.

What to Do When Friends Fail

To explore more of what the Bible has to say about this topic, consider the following passages:

• Psalm 55:12 – 14 and 20 – 21 describe David's shock over a betrayal by his close friend.

• Galatians 6:1 – 5 talks about bearing with the failures of our friends.

- The short book of Philemon encourages reconciliation of friendship after experiencing a difficult conflict.

CHAPTER 6

Falling in Love without Losing Your Mind Exercises

What's Your Love I.Q.?

This exercise will take about five or ten minutes. If you honestly answer the following items, you will have a clearer understanding of your "love smarts."

Would you say that you choose love or that love chooses you?

Love Chooses Me   I Choose Love

Are you likely to date almost anyone rather than to go without a date at all?

Almost Anyone   Go Without

Do you have a clear understanding of what qualities and character traits you want in the person you date, or are you more likely to discover that along the way?

Discover It along the Way   Know What I Want

Do you tend to make decisions based more on the way you feel or on the way you think?

Feeling   Thinking

If a person you are physically attracted to holds values and convictions that blatantly conflict with yours, are you more likely to explore the dating relationship or move on?

Explore   Move On

6 Falling in Love without Losing Your Mind Exercises

If you really like the person, but after a few dates he or she show signs of disrespecting you, are you able to see what's going on and let that person know it, or are you more likely to keep quiet and put up with it?

Keep Quiet and Put Up With It   See It and Talk about It

When it comes to physical passion, are you able to set your own boundaries and stay under control, or are you more likely to let your date call all the shots?

Let My Date Set the Speed   Set Boundaries and Keep Them

Do you believe in love at first sight or slowly simmering love?

First-Sight Love   Slow-Growth Love

Scoring Procedure: Tally your score to determine where you rank on the following level:

> 37–56   Above Average Love I.Q.
>
> 25–36   Average Love I.Q.
>
> 7–24   Below Average Love I.Q.

The point of this exercise is to help you assess your natural present inklings when it comes to dating relationships. Don't be discouraged by your score if it falls below average. This simply means that you may have more to gain from the principles discussed in this chapter of the book.

Are You a Good Match?

This exercise can take about five minutes and will help you determine whether the person you are dating possesses qualities and characteristics that fit the bill for you in the long run.

For each of the items in the following list, make a check mark for those qualities, traits, skills, or characteristics you possess in common with your dating partner.

THINGS WE HAVE IN COMMON

☐ Age

☐ Dependability

☐ Sense of humor

☐ Sincerity

☐ Religious convictions

☐ Family backgrounds

☐ Ability to adjust to things beyond your control

☐ Level of education

☐ Roles of women and men

☐ Political views

☐ Patience

☐ Use of alcohol and drugs

☐ Preference in music and entertainment

☐ Expression of emotions

☐ Management of anger

☐ Hobbies and activities

☐ Attitudes toward money

☐ Generosity

☐ Social skills

☐ Humility

☐ Hygiene standards

☐ Optimism

☐ Self-discipline and self-control

There is no numeric score for this exercise. The checklist is simply a tool for helping you see how much or how little you have in common with a person you are dating.

The True You Self-Test

This exercise will take about five minutes and will help you assess whether you are more likely to determine for yourself who you will be or whether you are more likely to be influenced by outside forces. Indicate your level of agreement for each of the following items.

1. I often feel helpless in dealing with the problems of life.
   - ☐ Strongly Agree
   - ☐ Agree
   - ☐ Disagree
   - ☐ Strongly Disagree

2. What happens to me in the future mostly depends on me.
   - ☐ Strongly Agree
   - ☐ Agree
   - ☐ Disagree
   - ☐ Strongly Disagree

3. I have little control over the things that happen to me.
   - ☐ Strongly Agree
   - ☐ Agree
   - ☐ Disagree
   - ☐ Strongly Disagree

4. There is really no way I can solve some of the problems I have.
   - ☐ Strongly Agree
   - ☐ Agree
   - ☐ Disagree
   - ☐ Strongly Disagree

5. I can do just about anything I really set my mind to.

☐ Strongly Agree

☐ Agree

☐ Disagree

☐ Strongly Disagree

6. Sometimes I feel that I'm being pushed around in life.

☐ Strongly Agree

☐ Agree

☐ Disagree

☐ Strongly Disagree

7. There is little I can do to change many of the important things in my life.

☐ Strongly Agree

☐ Agree

☐ Disagree

☐ Strongly Disagree

The preceding statements are designed to measure how much you have a sense of mastery and control over your life. Agreement with items 2 and 5 and disagreement with the remaining items indicate that you have what psychologists call an "internal locus of control" — that is, the belief that you are in control of and responsible for what happens in your life. Disagreement with items 2 and 5 and agreement with the remaining items indicate an "external locus of control" — the belief that what happens to you is determined by chance and that you are not responsible. These items cannot be considered the definitive test of your locus of control, but they can help you think about your own sense of taking responsibility and being true to yourself.

While the desire to be something or someone you are not may be tempting when trying to woo someone, it almost always spells disaster. For this reason, a stronger internal locus means you are more likely to be true to yourself.

Determining Your Bottom Line

This exercise will take about ten minutes and will help you uncover what you will and will not live with in a dating relationship. Take a moment to respond to each of the following questions. And remember, everyone's bottom line is different. So don't answer for anyone else but yourself.

When it comes to common courtesy from your dating partner, what do you expect?

When it comes to seeing other people during different stages of a dating relationship, where do you draw the line?

When it comes to expressing physical intimacy, where do you draw the line?

When it comes to personal values, religious beliefs, and spirituality, where do you draw the line?

Falling in Love without Losing Your Mind

To explore more of what the Bible has to say about this topic, consider the following passages:

• Genesis 29:18 tells the story of Jacob falling in love with Rachel.

• Judges 16 shows the serious consequences of Samson losing his mind as he falls in love with Delilah.

- Song of Solomon 8:6–7 talks about the powerful experience of being in love.

CHAPTER 7

Sex, Lies, and the Great Escape Exercises

EXERCISE 26

Your Most Important Sex Organ

This exercise can take as little as five minutes. But take your time to give serious consideration to the questions it poses.

Most people who "lose control" in the heat of the moment blame it on their hormones. "There's nothing I could have done to restrain myself," they say. What do you think? On the following scale rate how much control you think we human beings have over our sexual activity.

Total Control   No Control

1   2   3   4   5   6   7   8   9   10

If you circled 2 or higher, how do you explain your answer? Do you really believe that in a romantic relationship there comes a point where a couple simply can no longer control their physical attraction? That it is beyond their capacity to sexually restrain themselves? If you believe this, how do you substantiate your position?

Experts agree that human beings do have the capacity to be in total control of their sexual urges. Thanks to the cortex of our brain, we are different from animals. We can make decisions that govern how we will behave.

With this in mind, consider what you can do personally to turn on your brain power when you are faced with a strong temptation to give in to sexual urges. Be as specific and as practical as possible.

If you are comfortable sharing your ideas with another person, compare them with someone of the same gender.

The Bonds That Bind

This exercise will take about ten minutes. Emotional bonding — if it is to be healthy and long lasting — systematically progresses through some predictable stages. Research has revealed that the reason many relationships don't last is because the foundation for bonding is too often short-circuited. Take a moment to examine the following stages of physical intimacy:

1. Eye to body
2. Eye to eye
3. Voice to voice
4. Hand to hand
5. Hand to shoulder
6. Hand to waist
7. Face to face
8. Hand to head
9. Hand to body
10. Mouth to breast
11. Touching below the waist
12. Intercourse

As you review this progression of physical bonding, make note of how far your most intimate relationships have gone and how long it took you to get there. What were the consequences? You probably don't want to write down such personal information in this workbook, but you may want to jot down a few general thoughts on how moving prematurely through any of these stages may result in unhealthy consequences for a relationship. You might consider using a metaphor in articulating your thoughts (e.g., skipping a stage is like leaving a brick out of a foundation).

Ideally, how quickly (or slowly) do you personally think couples should progress through each stage? Make some notes next to each of the above stages. Do you have some thoughts on what might happen in any of these particular stages if they are experienced too quickly or even skipped altogether?

EXERCISE 28

Drawing the Line

This exercise will take about ten minutes and will help you answer some of the most important relationship questions you will ever ask. Where do you draw the line? Do you only kiss before getting married? Do you do anything as long as you both keep your pants on? What have you decided is right for you, and how do you stick to your decision? To help you explore and set boundaries in your intimate relationships, review the physical intimacy scale you read about in the book:

THE PHYSICAL INTIMACY SCALE

1. Embracing and hand holding
2. Cuddling and gentle caressing
3. Polite kissing on the lips
4. Passionate total mouth kissing
5. Intense and prolonged total mouth kissing
6. Fondling breasts and genitals outside the clothes
7. Fondling breasts and genitals under the clothes
8. Oral or genital stimulation to orgasm outside the clothes
9. Oral or genital stimulation to orgasm under the clothes
10. Genital intercourse

Again, you may not want to write this information here, but think about these questions. Where do you draw the line? Why?

7 Sex, Lies, and the Great Escape Exercises

95

What are the consequences of where you draw the line for you and your relationship (e.g., do you risk shutting off your sexuality completely; are you playing with fire; are you making intercourse inevitable)?

Once you have given this some thought and made a careful decision, consider what you will need to do to keep from crossing that line. This is a critically important step—and couples will get into trouble if it is not taken. So what practical things can you do to be sure you stick to your decision? What behaviors and what places do you need to avoid? What can you do in place of the risky behaviors? Consider a variety of scenarios and be as specific as possible.

Healing the Hurt of Sexual Regret

This exercise will take fifteen minutes or longer and is designed exclusively for readers who have made unhealthy sexual decisions and need to recover from the consequences. This may be a difficult exercise, but it is crucial to helping you find healing and getting a fresh start.

First, you need to recount in specific terms exactly what pain and hurt you carry with you from having sex too soon. What troubles you most about your experience? If you don't want to write in this book, find another place where you can record your feelings.

Once you have identified your heartache, you will need to take several steps to find your freedom from regret and pain. One of the best action plans we know of is found in Dick Purnell's book *Free to Love Again* (Thomas Nelson, 1989). Here are the steps he recommends:

1. Accept God's forgiveness.
2. Forgive yourself.
3. Expect powerful changes.
4. Guard your mind.
5. Dissolve immoral relationships.
6. Purify your passions.
7. Focus your future.

From the above list, which steps would seem to trip you up most and why?

Of course, a brief exercise in a workbook is not going to restore your spirit and erase your sexual regrets. This is only a start. Healing is always a process that takes time. So give yourself permission to be patient as you grieve and heal. In fact, we also recommend that you find someone — perhaps a trusted friend, a pastor, or a counselor — who can review the steps toward healing with you. Who could you turn to and trust with your story?

Don't put off this part of the plan. Having a competent confidant in this process is essential to helping you move beyond your pain and get a fresh start. You can get rid of guilt and find personal renewal.

Sex, Lies, and the Great Escape

To explore more of what the Bible has to say about this topic, consider the following passages:

- 1 Corinthians 6:18 – 20 talks about the painful impact of unwise sexual involvement in relationships.

- Galatians 5:19 – 21 talks about the emptiness of self-centered sexuality.

• Song of Solomon 1:1 – 4 celebrates the joy of sex.

CHAPTER 8

How to Break Up without Falling Apart Exercises

Is It Time to Break Up?

This exercise will take about ten minutes and will help you determine whether breaking up is a good idea in your situation.

The following list of reasons could all be arguably justifiable for causing a breakup. Take a moment to review these reasons and place a check mark next to any that apply to you and your relationship.

It may be time to break up if . . .

- ☐ The relationship is stifling you.
- ☐ The relationship is out of balance.
- ☐ You can't be yourself.
- ☐ You feel dominated and controlled.
- ☐ You've outgrown each other.
- ☐ You feel betrayed by his or her actions.
- ☐ You're more interested in someone else.
- ☐ Your values clash.
- ☐ You are waiting for your dating partner to change.
- ☐ This person doesn't help you become the kind of person you want to be.
- ☐ You don't feel physically safe around this person.
- ☐ You don't feel emotionally safe around this person.
- ☐ You give more than you receive in the relationship.
- ☐ You feel disrespected by this person.
- ☐ Your dating partner is involved in unhealthy behavior (e.g., drug abuse).
- ☐ You feel pressured by him or her to be someone you're not.

If you checked one or more of the items in this list, you need to carefully consider whether it is time to break up and move on. Consulting with an objective friend or counselor may help you clarify your thinking and make up your mind.

Making a Clean Break

This exercise will take about ten minutes and will help you clarify your own thinking on initiating a breakup.

Consider the situation: You've dated this person for more than a year and have discovered that your values clash and that you are feeling stifled by the relationship. You want to break up. From the following options, which response would you most likely choose?

☐ "What do you think about us just being friends?"

☐ "I really like you, but I need some time to think about our relationship."

☐ "I'm not comfortable in this relationship anymore and think it's better if we don't see each other."

The choice you made — understandably forced — in the above scenario may give you a quick glimpse into your general predisposition toward breaking up. If you chose the first response you are probably most likely to skirt the issue and end up with a painful, drawn-out breakup. If you chose the second response, you are probably aware of what you need to do but very hesitant to make a clean break. The final choice, though difficult to say, is probably the one that helps both of you make a clean break and move on.

Whatever your choice in the above situation, the following questions will help you explore issues that may give you personal insight into making you a better "breaker-upper."

• What is your biggest fear about initiating a breakup?

- Considering your situation, what is your idea of an ideal breakup? What would you say and how would it turn out?

Avoiding the Blame Game

This exercise will take about ten minutes and will help you assess the degree to which you may be blaming yourself for your breakup. Consider each of the following statements and use the scale to indicate how often each represents your thoughts. Take your time and be as honest as you can.

1 — Rarely or none of the time
2 — A little of the time
3 — Some of the time
4 — A good part of the time
5 — Most or all of the time

_____ I believe I could have done a lot more to prevent the breakup.

_____ I believe I am responsible for the breakup.

_____ I worry about what this person thinks of me.

_____ I need to take a hard look at myself.

_____ I feel ashamed as a result of the breakup.

_____ I detest myself for allowing the breakup to happen.

_____ I think that if I changed I could win this person back.

_____ I blame myself for the breakup.

_____ I keep thinking about how I could have done things differently.

_____ I wish I could turn back time and do things differently.

TOTAL SCORE X 2 = _____

Scoring: Add up your item scores and multiply your total by two. This provides a possible maximum score of up to 100. Use the following to interpret your score.

90-100 You are wracked with feelings of self-blame and punishment over being "rejected" by this person. You could probably benefit from help by a professional counselor to help you see reality more objectively in order to move beyond your pain.

80-89 You may not be in immediate need of professional help, but you aren't out of the danger zone. You need to process your feelings with a trusted friend or counselor and recognize the potential you have to suffer from serious self-punishment.

10-79 You are on your way to escaping the guilt trap. While your twinges of self-punishment are no doubt painful, you are most likely experiencing the common and natural feelings that many have after suffering a breakup. You will want to take special care not to allow self-blame to fester when it does appear.

Moving On

This exercise can take about ten minutes to much longer, and it will help you move beyond your grief of experiencing your breakup.

Take a moment to review the section of this chapter in the book that outlines Elisabeth Kübler-Ross's steps of grief and loss. In the space provided below, note how you have or are experiencing each phase. Write about your feelings during these times, and note some specific examples of what you experienced during each of them.

• Denial

• Anger

- Bargaining

- Depression

- Acceptance

How to Break Up without Falling Apart

To explore more of what the Bible has to say about this topic, consider the following passages:

• Psalm 34:18 tells of God's compassion for the brokenhearted.

• Psalm 69:20 voices the anguish of feelings that no one understands the pain of a broken heart.

- Psalm 102:23–28 tells of God's consistency even when everything else seems to be changing.

CHAPTER 9

Relating to God without Feeling Phony Exercises

Honest-to-Goodness Doubt

This exercise will take about ten minutes and will help you consider your faith and the degree to which you struggle with doubt. On the following continuums, circle the number that indicates where you stand. Be as honest in your responses as you can be.

My "faith" is nonexistent.   My faith is rock solid.

1   2   3   4   5   6   7   8   9   10

I don't know God.   I know God personally.

1   2   3   4   5   6   7   8   9   10

The Bible is just another book.   The Bible is a holy book inspired by God.

1   2   3   4   5   6   7   8   9   10

Jesus was simply an historical figure.   Jesus is my personal Savior.

1   2   3   4   5   6   7   8   9   10

God doesn't hear my prayers.   God hears and answers my prayers.

1   2   3   4   5   6   7   8   9   10

As you consider where you stand on the above continuums, take a moment to summarize your faith in a single sentence.

Now take a moment to summarize your doubt in a single sentence.

Will the Real God Please Stand Up?

This exercise can take about ten minutes and will help you uncover any misconceptions or distorted beliefs you have about God. Take a moment to review the passage in this chapter that ponders the question "Who is God?" Consider the four distorted concepts of God that are mentioned and indicate how often you view God in these ways.

	Rarely	Sometimes	Often
The Referee God	_____	_____	_____
The Grandfather God	_____	_____	_____
The Scientist God	_____	_____	_____
The Bodyguard God	_____	_____	_____

From the above list of distortions, which one are you most likely to view and why? If none of these four distortions is likely to trip you up, how do you sometimes misunderstand God's character?

Now consider what may be one of the most difficult questions you have ever pondered: Who is God to you? Take a moment to write a brief paragraph on this topic. Consider the traits and qualities that come to mind when you think about who God is.

Does God Really Love Me?

This exercise will take about ten minutes and will help you assess the degree to which you experience God's love at a personal level. Consider each of the following statements and use the scale to indicate how often each represents your beliefs. Take your time and be as honest as you can.

1 — Rarely or none of the time
2 — A little of the time
3 — Some of the time
4 — A good part of the time
5 — Most or all of the time

_____ I believe that nothing could ever separate me from God's love.

_____ I am aware of how special I am to God.

_____ I believe that God is love.

_____ God's grace permeates my life.

_____ I'm confident that God loves me so much that he sacrificed his only Son in my place.

_____ I believe God loves me as if I were the only person on earth.

_____ I am free from irrational guilt feelings because of God's love.

_____ I believe I can do nothing to earn God's love because it is given freely.

_____ I know God loves me.

_____ I can love others because God first loved me.

TOTAL SCORE X 2 = _____

Scoring: Add up your item scores and multiply your total by two. This provides a possible maximum score of up to 100.

Use the following to interpret your score.

90–100 You have a solid and secure understanding of how much God loves you.

80–89   You may experience some ambivalence at times about how much God loves you, but deep down you rest in knowing that he does love you.

10–79   You are struggling to know whether God loves you or not. If your score is below 60, you would certainly benefit from counsel on God's grace.

Really Relating to God

This exercise can take as little as ten minutes to much longer, and it is designed to help you formulate how you relate to God and how you wish you related to God—and what you can do to move in that direction. This final workbook exercise may appear relatively simple at first, but it is probably the most difficult of all.

In a single sentence, summarize your faith journey and how it has brought you to your present relationship with God. Then note a few key descriptors of your present relationship with God.

Now, take a moment to consider how you might represent your present relationship with God by drawing a simple picture of it. Be as creative as you like.

Once you have completed your pictorial representation of this relationship, consider what you would like to change to make it more like the relationship you long for. What would those changes involve?

What can you do, in practical terms, to make that kind of relationship with God a reality?

Relating to God without Feeling Phony

To explore more of what the Bible has to say about this topic, consider the following passages:

• Ephesians 3:16 – 19 talks about the experience of knowing God deeply.

• Psalm 139 talks about the intimate way God knows us.

• John 15:1 – 15 talks about the intimate relationship we have with God through Christ.

For Group Discussion
with the Accompanying DVD

Introduction to your Small Group Study

Studying this material in a small group with other people is one of the best ways to make it stick—and have a lot of fun in the process.

This small group discussion is designed to be used with the accompanying DVD kit. You can order this DVD at *www.RealRelationships.com*.

In the following pages you will find discussion questions you can use in each of your six small group sessions. Don't get hung up on answering every one of them in order. Use the questions that work best for the personality of your group.

You will see that not all chapters in the book are covered in these sessions. Why? Because most groups feel that six sessions is just about the right length for a small group series. Of course, you can feel free to bring into your group discussions the content you'd like to explore for the chapters that are not highlighted in your six sessions.

Obviously, you are going to get more out of the discussion if you've read the pertinent chapters. But if you haven't read them, don't worry. You can still join in on the discussion and you don't need to feel an ounce of guilt. The purpose is to enjoy the interaction and learn from it. You can read the chapters later on if you wish.

You'll also find that each of the sessions will rely on an exercise or two from this workbook. We've selected exercises that will not put anyone on the spot or force anyone to share information they don't want to. Of course, your group may elect to use other exercises from this workbook to discuss if you wish. That's up to you and your group.

A key ingredient to successful small group discussion is vulnerability. Typically, the more transparent you are, the more meaningful the experience will be. And the more open others will be as well. Vulnerability begets vulnerability.

Another key ingredient in these discussions is specificity. You'll gain much more out of this time when you use specific examples from your life. So with this in mind, we will remind you to "be specific" every so often.

One more thing. Each session begins with a question that is "just for fun"—a kind of icebreaker. They are just to get the wheels turning as you come together as a group.

So relax. Have fun. And learn all you can to enjoy more fully the gifts of Real Relationships.

Your Compulsion for Completion

Just for Fun (5 minutes)

Name one unusual talent you have or a unique experience you've had that most people wouldn't know about you until they "really" got to know you.

Video Notes (10 minutes)

Discussion Questions (20 minutes)

The following questions are to help facilitate a meaningful small group discussion. Feel free to explore different territory if you like. The goal is to connect as a group and process the information from Chapter 1 of *Real Relationships* together. In the space provided, jot down your own thoughts as well as some of the group's responses to these questions. And remember, anyone is always free to "pass" on any particular question without explanation.

1. Describe your experience of completing the exercises for this chapter. What did you learn about yourself?

2. What do you make of the idea that it is only when we no longer compulsively need someone that we can ever attempt to build a healthy relationship with them? Do you agree? Why or why not?

3. Of the two lies discussed in this chapter, which do you encounter more often (if you *had* to choose one): (1) I need this person to be complete; or (2) If this person needs me, I'll be complete?

4. It's easy to rely on another person instead of God to meet your deepest needs. Why do you think most of us struggle with this idea?

TALKING THROUGH YOUR EXERCISE:
Small Group Insights (30 minutes)

Since this exercise requires that each group member complete the online questionnaire before coming to the group (and bringing their personal report with them), be sure to sync up with your group in advance to expedite this. If not, you can do this at your next group meeting.

Take time to explore the results of your online Small Group Insights Profile. You received a complimentary code to use this tool if you purchased a copy of *RealRelationships*. But if you don't have a copy of the book you can still obtain your personal report for a very nominal fee at the website: **www.SmallGroupInsights.com**. It takes about ten minutes to complete the questionnaire.

The report comes with three built-in exercises to help you share your own results and learn about others in your group:

1. Sharing My Group Style

2. Going Deeper with My Personal Style

3. My Personal Communication Preferences

While you can do this in as little as twenty-five minutes, you may find that you want to spend more time on this. The tool, after all, is designed to heighten your personal insight and help you bond as a group. In short, it fosters "real relationships." So be sure to set aside thirty minutes or so to explore the results of your reports together.

TALKING THROUGH YOUR EXERCISE:
Taking Off Your Masks (10 to 15 minutes)

If you haven't done so already, take time right now to complete Exercise 3 in this workbook, "Taking Off Your Masks." This exercise will help you identify some of the masks you might wear on occasion. Once each member of the group has completed the exercise, take turns exploring your answers together and answer the following question:

• How willing and comfortable are you to disclose yourself to others and let yourself be known by others? What social masks do you sometimes wear that guard you against being vulnerable? When are you most likely to wear them?

Keeping Family Ties
from Pulling Strings

Just for Fun (5 minutes)

As a group, name as many movies as you can that feature families. Next, identify one of your personal favorite "family movies" and why you chose it.

Video Notes (10 minutes)

Discussion Questions (20 minutes)

The following questions are to help facilitate a meaningful small group discussion. Feel free to explore different territory, but don't veer too far off track. In the space provided, jot down some of the group's responses, as well as your own, to these questions. And remember, anyone is always free to "pass" on any particular question without explanation.

1. Describe your experience of completing the exercises for this chapter. What did you learn about yourself?

2. Can you think of another social force that has had more power in shaping your life than the family? Why or why not?

3. In what specific ways has your family of origin shaped your personality, your career choice, your relationships, your values? Be specific.

4. In what specific ways does your family still "pull your strings"? In other words, how do your early family influences still manifest themselves in your present relationships?

5. Of the three major ways families shape us—rules, roles, and relationships—which one do you see as the most influential and why? Can you think of an example to underscore your reasoning?

TALKING THROUGH YOUR EXERCISE:
Uncovering Unspoken Rules (15 minutes)

If you haven't done so already, take time right now to complete Exercise 6 in this workbook, "Uncovering Unspoken Rules." This exercise will help you identify some of the rules that continue to shape your relationships even now. Once each member of the group has completed the exercise, take turns exploring your answers together.

TALKING THROUGH YOUR EXERCISE:
Revisit Small Group Insights (10 minutes)

Take a moment before your group ends this session to see if there are any after-thoughts regarding your last session and the results of your online report (from **www.SmallGroupInsights.com**). Have you had any new awareness or insights regarding your personal style since your last session? Take a moment to share these with each other.

Bridging the Gender Gap

Just for Fun (5 minutes)

If you were to compare and contrast the attitudes or behaviors of the opposite gender to a space alien that had never seen or heard of them, what would you say? What adjectives would you use?

Video Notes (10 minutes)

Discussion Questions (20 minutes)

The following questions are to help facilitate a meaningful small group discussion. Feel free to explore different territory, but don't veer too far off track. In the space provided, jot down some of the group's responses to these questions. And remember, anyone is always free to "pass" on any particular question without explanation.

1. Describe your experience of completing the exercises for this chapter. What did you learn about yourself?

2. Consider your cross-gender relationships. What aspects of these relationships with the opposite sex (excluding romantic relationships) seem to be easier than relationships with the same sex? What are the biggest hurdles you encounter in relating with the opposite sex?

3. When you were growing up as a kid, what social activities or games do you think influenced your gender roles? Looking back on it, do you put more stock in the way your environment shaped you or the way your biology programmed you?

4. This chapter notes several things men and women should know about the opposite gender. Do you agree with them? What differences could you add?

5. Have you noticed how women use their conversation to build "rapport" while men use conversation to give or get the "report"? What examples of this disparity can you remember from your own experience?

6. The major point of this chapter is that we doom our relationships with the opposite sex when we try to change them into being more like us. If this is so, what can you do to accept and even appreciate the different qualities of the other gender?

TALKING THROUGH YOUR EXERCISE:
What If You Were the Opposite Sex? (30 minutes)

If you haven't done so already, take time right now to complete Exercise 10 in this workbook, "What If You Were the Opposite Sex?" This exercise will lead you through an experience of empathy for the opposite gender. It's an eye opener. Once each member of the group has completed the exercise, take turns exploring your experiences and your answers to the exercise questions together.

Friends to Die For

Just for Fun (5 minutes)

Describe your very first good friendship — from when you were a little kid. Who was it with and why was it special? Do you still know them?

Video Notes (10 minutes)

Discussion Questions (20 minutes)

The following questions are to help facilitate a meaningful small group discussion. Feel free to explore different territory, but don't veer too far off track. In the space provided, jot down some of the group's responses to these questions. And remember, anyone is always free to "pass" on any particular question without explanation.

1. Describe your experience of completing the exercises for this chapter. What did you learn about yourself?

2. It has been said that many people audition to be our friends but only a few make the cut. What is it about your friends that caused them to get the part? Did it have more to do with circumstances or personal qualities?

3. The medical benefits of having friends are quite remarkable. What benefits of the less scientific kind do you appreciate? What fruits of friendship do you enjoy the most?

4. Do you agree that generally speaking, our good friends come in two forms: as friends of the road and friends of the heart? Think of an example of a meaningful friendship that did not last. What purpose did it serve in your life or what passage did it see you through?

5. Forgiveness can be one of the most challenging struggles for any relationship. Think of a time when you were either on the receiving or the giving end of forgiveness. What makes it so difficult?

6. Of the four qualities that keep friendships going — loyalty, forgiveness, honesty, and dedication — which one is most important to you and why? What other qualities would you add to this list?

TALKING THROUGH YOUR EXERCISE:
Are You a "Growth Promoting" Listener? (30 minutes)

If you haven't done so already, take time right now to complete Exercise 14 in this workbook, "Are You a 'Growth Promoting' Listener?" This exercise will lead you to explore a quality most of us need to continually improve and hone. What are your strengths and areas for improvement when it comes to this essential friendship quality? Once each member of the group has completed the exercise, take turns exploring your answers in this exercise together.

Improving Your Love I.Q.

Just for Fun (5 minutes)

What's the best or the worst piece of advice you've ever heard when it comes to romantic love?

Video Notes (10 minutes)

Discussion Questions (20 minutes)

The following questions are to help facilitate a meaningful small group discussion. Feel free to explore different territory, but don't veer too far off track. In the space provided, jot down some of the group's responses to these questions. And remember, anyone is always free to "pass" on any particular question without explanation.

1. Describe your experience of completing the exercises for this chapter. What did you learn about yourself?

2. In specific terms, how would you describe the emotions surrounding infatuation and falling in love? Are they the same thing?

3. Journalist Helen Rowland said, "Falling in love consists merely in uncorking the imagination and bottling the common sense." In what ways does falling in love impair our judgment and deplete our common sense?

4. Do you agree that detecting your partner's values can be one of the smartest moves you make while dating? Why or why not? If you believe it is important, how do you go about discovering them?

5. If you are willing to share with the group, how have you tried to change another person to please you more? And how have you tried to change yourself to please another person? In both cases, what was the result?

6. What "bottom lines" have you determined for yourself in dating other people? Do you need to communicate them to the person you are dating? If so, how do you do this?

TALKING THROUGH YOUR EXERCISE:
What's Your Love I.Q.? (30 minutes)

If you haven't done so already, take time right now to complete Exercise 22 in this workbook, "What's Your Love I.Q.?" This self-test will provide a little snap shot of your thinking about dating and romance. Once each member of the group has completed the exercise, take turns exploring your answers in this exercise together. Of course, this can be a very personal matter so be sure to treat each other with care and sensitivity.

Relating to God without Feeling Phony

Just for Fun (5 minutes)

As you review our past twenty-four hours, when would you say that you felt closest to God and why?

Video Notes (10 minutes)

Discussion Questions (20 minutes)

The following questions are to help facilitate a meaningful small group discussion. Feel free to explore different territory, but don't veer too far off track. In the space provided, jot down some of the group's responses to these questions. And remember, anyone is always free to "pass" on any particular question without explanation.

1. Describe your experience of completing the exercises for this chapter. What did you learn about yourself?

2. Does doubt have any place in an authentic relationship with God? Why or why not? Do you believe that doubt can help a person find a faith of her own? If so, how?

3. The chapter mentions a few misperceptions people often have about who God is. Do you identify with any of these? If so, how? If not, what misperceptions of God's character have you experienced?

4. If someone were to ask you why a person needs God, what would you say and why?

5. In specific terms, how do you see God as the only one who can truly fulfill our compulsion for completion? If you don't agree with this position, why not?

6. What does it mean to you when this chapter says the only way to relate to God without feeling phony is to do so with integrity? What does integrity mean to you?

TALKING THROUGH YOUR EXERCISE:
Will the Real God Please Stand Up? (10 minutes)

If you haven't done so already, take time right now to complete Exercise 35 in this workbook, "Will the Real God Please Stand Up?" This exercise will help you explore your relationship with God—especially any distorted beliefs that might be impairing your relationship. Once each member of the group has completed the exercise, take turns exploring your answers in this exercise together.

TALKING THROUGH YOUR EXERCISE:
Revisit Small Group Insights (10 minutes)

Remember the online questionnaire you took at the beginning of this study (from **www.SmallGroupInsights.com)**? Review your results right now and consider how your personal style (as either a Talker, Thinker, Listener, or Doer) shapes your relationship with God. Take a moment to share your thoughts with each other.

SMALL GROUP INSIGHTS

Where Real Relationships Start

Successful small group experiences depend on authentic relationships. The better the connections, the better the group. And that's just what this tool will do for you.

- Simple
- Personalized
- Engaging
- Quick

Whatever your group's purpose, the Small Group Insights Profile provides you with a fast-track to authenticity and meaningful connection.

www.smallgroupinsights.com

The Complete Guide to Marriage Mentoring

Connecting Couples to Build Better Marriages

Drs. Les and Leslie Parrott

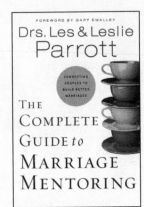

A comprehensive resource to help churches build a thriving marriage mentoring program.

Les and Leslie Parrott are passionate about how marriage mentoring can transform couples, families, and entire congregations. *The Complete Guide to Marriage Mentoring* includes life-changing insights and essential skills for

- Preparing engaged and newlywed couples
- Maximizing marriages from good to great
- Repairing marriages in distress

Practical guidelines help mentors and couples work together as a team, agree on outcomes, and develop skills for the marriage mentoring process. Appendixes offer a wealth of additional resources and tools. An exhaustive resource for marriage mentorship in any church setting, this guide also includes insights from interviews with church leaders and marriage mentors from around the country.

"The time is ripe for marriage mentoring, and this book is exactly what we need."

— Gary Smalley, author of *The DNA of Relationships*

Available in stores and online!

Saving Your Marriage Before It Starts

Seven Questions to Ask Before—and After—You Marry

Drs. Les and Leslie Parrott

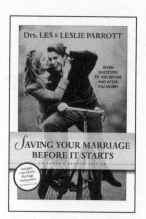

Saving Your Marriage Before It Starts, created by relationship experts Drs. Les and Leslie Parrott, is a comprehensive marriage program designed specifically for today's couples by a couple. And now, in this updated edition, the Parrotts' award-winning approach has been expanded to incorporate ten more years of feedback, research, and professional experience.

This is more than a book—it's practically a self-guided premarital counseling course, and it is used by counselors and churches across the country and, now in ten languages, worldwide. Questions at the end of every chapter help you explore each topic personally. Companion men's and women's workbooks* full of self-tests and exercises help you apply what you learn and enjoy intimate discussions along the way. There is even a seven-session DVD kit (with a bonus session for people entering a second marriage) available that you can use on your own or with other couples in a group or a class that want to grow together. In this dynamic DVD you'll not only hear entertaining and insightful teaching from the Parrotts, but you'll also meet other real-life couples who provide amazing candor and perspective.

Relationship experts Les and Leslie Parrott show you the secrets to building a marriage that lasts.

- Uncover the most important misbeliefs of marriage
- Learn how to communicate with instant understanding
- Discover the secret to reducing and resolving conflict
- Master the skills of money management
- Get your sex life off to a great start
- Understand the three essential ingredients to lasting love
- Discover the importance of becoming "soul mates" ... and more.

Make your marriage everything it is meant to be. Save your marriage—before (and after) it starts.

Saving Your Second Marriage Before It Starts

Nine Questions to Ask Before (and After) You Remarry

Drs. Les and Leslie Parrott

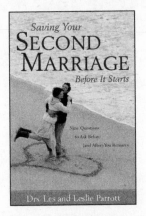

Sixty percent of second marriages fail. Yours can be among the ones that succeed. Relationship experts Les and Leslie Parrott show how you can beat the odds with flying colors and make remarriage the best thing that's ever happened to you. Do you have the skills you need? Now is the time to acquire them — and build a future together that is everything marriage can and ought to be.

Also available: men's workbook, women's workbook, and audio download version

Available in stores and online!

Love Talk

Speak Each Other's Language Like You Never Have Before

Drs. Les and Leslie Parrott

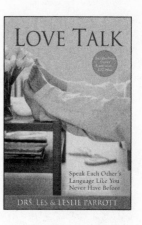

A breakthrough discovery in communication for transforming love relationships.

Over and over, couples consistently name "improved communication" as the greatest need in their relationships. *Love Talk*, by acclaimed relationship experts Drs. Les and Leslie Parrott, is a deep yet simple plan full of new insights that will revolutionize communication in love relationships.

In this no-nonsense book, "psychobabble" is translated into easy-to-understand language that clearly teaches you what you need to do — and not do — in order to speak each other's language like you never have before.

Love Talk includes:

- The Love Talk Indicator, a free personalized online assessment (a $30.00 value) to help you determine your unique talk style
- The Secret to Emotional Connection
- Charts and sample conversations
- The most important conversation you'll ever have
- A short course on Communication 101
- Appendix on Practical Help for the "Silent Partner"

Two softcover his and hers workbooks are full of lively exercises and enlightening self-tests that help couples apply what they are learning about communication directly to their relationships.

Available in stores and online!

Trading Places

The Secret to the Marriage You Want

Drs. Les and Leslie Parrott

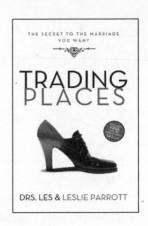

To understand your spouse you've got to walk in his or her shoes.

Ever feel like you're stepping on each other's toes? Then maybe it's time you put yourselves in each other's shoes. Of course that may sound uncomfortable. But it's easier than you think — and it will revolutionize your relationship. In fact, bestselling authors Drs. Les and Leslie Parrott reveal the little-known secrets of putting the time-tested strategy of trading places to work in your own marriage.

In this book, chock-full of practical helps and tips you've never thought of, you'll learn the three-step-strategy to trading places and, as a result, you're sure to:

- Increase your levels of passion
- Bolster your commitment
- Eliminate nagging

- Short-circuit conflict
- Double your laughter
- Forgive more quickly
- Talk more intimately

This book also features a powerful, free online assessment that instantly improves your inclination to trade places.

Most couples never discover the rewards of trading places. For example, did you know it's the quickest way to get your own needs met? It's true! And Les and Leslie show you how. They also disclose exactly how trading places improves your conversations and how it's guaranteed to fire up your sex life. Truly, your love life and your entire marriage will never be the same after you learn the intimate dance of trading places.

Available in stores and online!

Crazy Good Sex

Putting to Bed the Myths Men Have about Sex

Dr. Les Parrott

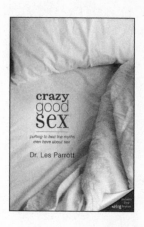

The combustive force of a man's sexual drive can incinerate his wedding vows and family commitments — or it can ignite a flame of passion within his marriage that brings mind-blowing pleasure to both partners.

In this practical guidebook filled with straight talk about the issues that concern men, psychologist Dr. Les Parrott reveals the truth about six areas that can undermine a man's confidence, damage his marriage, and leave him struggling unnecessarily with temptation.

Parrott counters these false beliefs and uncovers the answers to:

- how much sex women want
- whether married sex can be truly satisfying and steamy
- the biological effects of pornography
- what it really takes to please a woman
- whether masturbation is harmful or helpful
- the controlling force behind a man's sexual drive

Readers will learn how to change both their beliefs and their behavior, paving the way for a whole new dimension of sexual pleasure.

Available in stores and online!

Share Your Thoughts

With the Author: Your comments will be forwarded to the author when you send them to *zauthor@zondervan.com*.

With Zondervan: Submit your review of this book by writing to *zreview@zondervan.com*.

Free Online Resources at
www.zondervan.com

Zondervan AuthorTracker: Be notified whenever your favorite authors publish new books, go on tour, or post an update about what's happening in their lives at www.zondervan.com/authortracker.

Daily Bible Verses and Devotions: Enrich your life with daily Bible verses or devotions that help you start every morning focused on God. Visit www.zondervan.com/newsletters.

Free Email Publications: Sign up for newsletters on Christian living, academic resources, church ministry, fiction, children's resources, and more. Visit www.zondervan.com/newsletters.

Zondervan Bible Search: Find and compare Bible passages in a variety of translations at www.zondervanbiblesearch.com.

Other Benefits: Register to receive online benefits like coupons and special offers, or to participate in research.

ZONDERVAN

ZONDERVAN.com/
AUTHORTRACKER
follow your favorite authors